ALAMO!

Other Scholastic Paperbacks You Will Enjoy:

ALAMO!

GEORGE SULLIVAN

SCHOLASTIC INC.

New York   Toronto   London   Auckland   Sydney

ISBN 0-590-50313-8

12 11 10 9 8 7 6 5 4 3 2 1   7 8 9/9 0 1 2/0

Printed in the U.S.A.   34

First Scholastic printing, March 1997

Acknowledgments

The author is grateful to the many archivists, historians, collection curators, and librarians who provided background information and artwork for use in this book. Special thanks are due staff members of the Texas History Research Library at the Alamo, including Wallace Saage, curator; Cathy Herpich, library director; Martha Utterback, Charles Gamez, and Linda Edwards. Special thanks are also due Diane H. Bruce, librarian, and Tom Shelton, photographs archivist, The University of Texas Institute of Texan Cultures, San Antonio; Les Smith, audio visual director, San Jacinto Museum of History; John Anderson, preservation officer, Texas State Library; Maya Keech, Prints and Photographs, Library of Congress; Dr. Gilberto Hinojosa, Incarnate Word College; Cahndice E. Matthews, Esparza Elementary School, San Antonio; Sal Alberti and James Lowe, James Lowe Autographs; Edwin M. Eakin, Eakin Press; Anita Arndt, Steck-Vaughn Co.; Francesca Kurti, TLC Labs; Tim Sullivan, Frederick Ray, Anthony Barboza, Claudia Carlson, and Danal Terry.

CONTENTS

ALAMO!

CHAPTER 1

WHICH ALAMO TO REMEMBER?

It ranks as one of the most dramatic battles of all time. A band of fewer than 200 rebels sought to defend what had been a Spanish mission in San Antonio against thousands of Mexican troops under General Santa Anna.

A bloodbath was the result. The Mexicans' final assault at just after dawn on March 6, 1836, killed every defender in about ninety minutes. Estimates of the Mexican dead range from about 600 to almost three times that number.

The story doesn't end there. Forty-six days after the battle, a ragtag force of Americans commanded by Sam Houston pounced upon Santa Anna's unwarned Mexican troops at San Jacinto. Crying "Remember the Alamo!" they overwhelmed the Mexicans and captured Santa Anna. The Mexican dictator was forced into signing a peace treaty granting Texas its independence.

"Remember the Alamo!"

Today that cry can still produce feelings of patriotism among many Americans. Grade-school students have

The Alamo, hailed as "The Shrine of Texas Liberty."

A monument honoring William Barret Travis, Davy Crockett, and other Alamo defenders stands in Alamo Plaza, just west of the Alamo itself.

At the Alamo's entrance, visitors are reminded to be respectful.

long been taught to look upon the one-time mission-fortress in what is now downtown San Antonio as "The Shrine of Texas Liberty." The Alamo's defenders, textbooks say, were fighting for freedom and democracy.

But this version of what happened at at the Alamo can create problems for Hispanic children. They're taught that the Mexicans are bad guys who killed Davy Crockett, Jim Bowie, and the other Alamo defenders. They see their ancestors cast as enemies. The fact that a good number of Mexican Texans — Tejanos — fought shoulder to shoulder with Crockett, Bowie, and the others is often overlooked.

As for the people of Mexico, they don't look upon the Alamo the way most Americans do. Texas, after all,

Toribio Losoya, one of the Alamo's Tejano defenders, was an unsung hero of the battle until recent times.

belonged to Mexico at the time of the siege. Many Mexicans see the Alamo as only one in a series of battles against an aggressive nation that was seeking to acquire new territory by force. Most of the Anglo-Americans who fought at the Alamo were foreigners in Mexico; they were illegal aliens.

"Remember the Alamo!"

Native Americans have still another point of view about the Alamo. To the Inter-Tribal Council of American Indians, the site is neither a shrine nor the symbol of an Anglo-American land grab. The Council looks upon the Alamo as a sacred cemetery for Native Americans and others who were converted to Christianity at the Spanish mission.

According to Council historical records, 921 mission Indians were buried near the Alamo between 1774 and 1821. The Tribal Council says that the Alamo is one of the nation's first integrated cemeteries. Not only Native Americans, but Hispanics, African-Americans, and whites are buried there.

As this suggests, remembering the Alamo in a real sense is no easy matter. Not everyone agrees on what happened there. That's because after the Alamo's fall, reports on what took place there were woven together in a story that mixed fact and fiction. Only recently have people begun to try to sort things out.

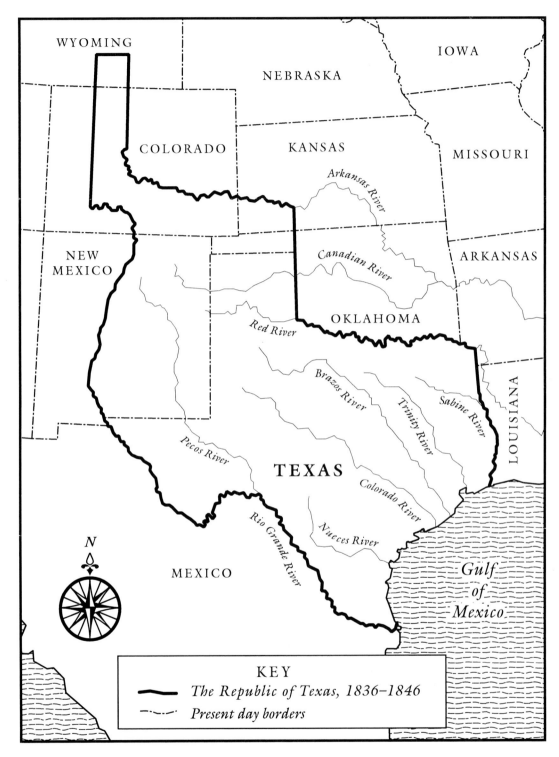

Boundary lines for the Republic of Texas in 1836 included parts of what is now Wyoming, Colorado, Kansas, New Mexico, and Oklahoma.

CHAPTER 2

THE FIRST TEXANS

The story of the Alamo begins in 1821, the year that Mexico won its freedom from Spain. With independence, Texas became a territory within the new empire of Mexico.

The portion of Mexico known as Texas was very big, much bigger than it is today. According to an 1819 treaty between Spain and the United States, the eastern border of the territory was marked by the Sabine River. The Rio Grande would later be named as the western border.

In 1836, after Texas declared its independence, the Republic of Texas claimed some 360,000 square miles, an area bigger by about 100,000 square miles than the state occupies today. Texas's boundaries then included

Young Stephen Austin took over his father's land grants and established the first colony of Anglo-Americans in Mexican Texas.

parts of what is now Wyoming, Colorado, Kansas, New Mexico, and Oklahoma.

Texas was bigger than France, bigger than Spain, and twice as big as Germany. Texas was more than one-third the geographical size of what was then the United States.

Texas had land — and relatively small numbers of people. Apart from Native Americans, only a few thousand Mexicans lived there.

All that empty land tempted Americans.

One of the first Americans to seek to colonize Texas was fifty-nine-year-old Moses Austin, an energetic Missouri banker. In 1820 Austin went to San Antonio de Béxar, then the capital of Texas. Because Mexico sought both to control and to populate Texas by the *empresario* system, Austin had to ask Spanish officials for permission to establish a colony of 300 American families in the territory. These families paid small fees for land and agreed to live under Mexican law. Early the next year, the Spanish approved his request.

When Moses Austin died in 1821, his son, Stephen Fuller Austin, took over the grant. Quiet, college-educated, a born leader, Austin settled the colonists in San Felipe de Austin and Columbia, on the Brazos River in southeast Texas, some 175 miles northeast of San Antonio de Béxar. Austin described his settlement as "… good in every respect a man could wish for… land, all first rate, plenty of lumber, fine water… " Each man received 640 acres.

After Mexico gained its independence from Spain, Austin got permission from the Mexican government to continue the project. While other Americans asked for and received Mexican land grants, none was as successful as Austin. The first Anglo-Americans to establish homes and raise families in Texas, Austin's colony eventually numbered more than a thousand families — farmers from Kentucky and Tennessee, cotton growers from Alabama and Georgia, and artisans from New York.

The news of Mexico's generous land policies spread across the South and throughout the Mississippi Valley. Broadsides proclaiming Texas's glories were posted in town squares and advertisements placed in newspapers.

While it meant free land and a fresh start, Texas wasn't for everyone. Texas was a harsh frontierland with often hostile Indians. It was a land to be tamed. Few women made the trek.

When the first Europeans arrived in what is now Texas, they found the land occupied by several different Indian tribes, including the Karankawas, Tonkawas, and Caddos. They also encountered the Kiowas, who were Plains Indians of the southwestern U.S. White Bear (San-tan-ta) was a Kiowa chief from 1869 to 1874.

Under Spanish rule, Texas had been a separate state. But when Mexico became a republic in 1824, Texas's status changed. Texas was joined together with the province of Coahuila to form the state of Coahuila y Texas. Texas thus lost its separate identity. In addition, the Mexican government moved the capital from San Antonio de Béxar to Saltillo, more than 300 miles to the southwest.

A law enacted the following year, 1825, gave individual Mexican states the right to set their own colonization policy. Coahuila y Texas took advantage of the new law, opening its border to American immigrants. The population mushroomed. By 1830, there were about 16,000 Anglo-Americans living in Texas. They called themselves Texians, and they outnumbered Tejanos by about four to one. Austin, in recruiting for his colonies, had made an effort to be selective, to choose responsible, hardworking families. They adapted to Mexican customs and Mexican law. But the newer immigrants had less patience and little respect for authority. Many of them looked upon Texas as a place of adventure, opportunity, or escape. Debtors, lawbreakers, and husbands seeking to break the bonds of marriage streamed into Texas.

Most Anglo-Americans from Southern states brought slaves with them to Texas,

"Lazooing a Horse on the Prairies" is the title of this print, an illustration from "A Visit to Texas," published in 1834.

although the practice of slavery was against Mexican law. But the newcomers saw no reason to give up any of the rights and privileges they had enjoyed in the United States. Bad feelings began to develop between the Anglo-Americans and the Mexican government.

In 1830 the Mexican government, afraid that Texas was becoming overwhelmed by the torrent of Anglo-Americans pouring across its borders, halted further immigration.

But Mexico lacked the soldiers to patrol its long border with the United States. Americans continued to flood into the territory.

At the same time, the Mexican government announced it would begin collecting fees and customs duties from the settlers. The money was needed to run the government. But the colonists had never paid such taxes before, and the new regulations angered them. Their discontent would soon lead to revolt.

CHAPTER 3

THE FIRST SHOTS

In 1833, as the links between the Mexican government and the Anglo-American settlers in Mexican Texas kept getting weaker and weaker, a trim, dark-haired general and politician named Antonio López de Santa Anna took control of Mexico. A brave man, but also a ruthless one, Santa Anna was to have a jolting effect on the lives of all Texans, Tejanos, and Anglo-Americans alike.

Born in Jalapa in Mexico in 1794, Santa Anna became a cadet in the Spanish army stationed in Mexico at the age of sixteen, and he later fought against the Mexicans who were resisting Spanish rule in the War of Independence. Before the war ended, Santa Anna deserted the Spanish and joined the Mexicans. Afterward, the victorious Mexicans named him military governor of Yucatán. Ambitious for wealth and fame, Santa Anna often declared, "Man is nothing; power is everything." There is no one to compare to Santa Anna in the history of the United States. He served as president of Mexico no fewer than

Antonio López de Santa Anna, president of Mexico and general-in-chief of the army, vowed to rout Texas's rebels.

eleven times between 1833 and 1855. Always he was overthrown.

Santa Anna had a very low opinion of the Anglo-Americans who had settled in Texas. To him they were land-grabbers and nothing more. He made up his mind to rout the rebels and keep Texas in Mexico's camp.

On April 1, 1833, the same day Santa Anna had taken over in Mexico, Stephen Austin and some fifty-five other delegates from every part of Texas met in San Felipe de Austin to draft a resolution that would define for Santa Anna their ideas on statehood. Most Anglo-Americans who had lived in Texas for any amount of time were still loyal to

General Martín Perfecto de Cós, Santa Anna's brother-in-law, sought to subdue rebels at Anahuac.

Mexico. The same was true for the Tejanos. What they wanted was for Texas to be disconnected from Coahuila and made a separate state. They wanted to be able to run their own affairs. Only the most radical of Anglos, the so-called War Dogs, sought independence for Texas. Their party was the War Party. Its members were mostly lawyers and land developers. For them, a free Texas would mean almost limitless opportunities for acquiring land and making money.

Once the San Felipe convention ended, the delegates agreed to send Austin to Mexico City to meet with Santa Anna. Austin carried with him a petition that requested Mexican statehood for Texas.

Several long and difficult months passed before Austin, a Federalist, was able to arrange a meeting with Santa Anna, a Centralist. Federalists supported the constitution of 1824; the Centralists wanted Mexico City to be powerful in all aspects. When Austin and Santa Anna finally met, the Mexican leader rejected the idea of statehood for Texas but granted some of Austin's other requests, including one that permitted immigration to be resumed.

Austin was in good spirits as he left for home. Then events took an unexpected turn. As he was making his way north, Austin was arrested for plotting to separate Texas from Mexico. He was brought back to Mexico City and thrown into jail. Austin would remain behind bars for a year and a half.

Meanwhile, Santa Anna was tightening his control. He, in effect, discarded

From their cannon, rebels hung their lone-star flag that proclaimed "Come and take it."

A zealous leader of the War Dogs, William Barret Travis commanded the rebels at Anahuac and later at the Alamo.

the liberal Mexican Constitution of 1824, replacing it with his own rule of law. In January 1835 Santa Anna sent his brother-in-law, Gen. Martín Perfecto de Cós, with an infantry battalion to Saltillo with orders to remove the government leaders there.

As General Cós was taking over in Saltillo, he received news that there was trouble to the north, in Texas. Santa Anna had ordered customs duties to be collected throughout Texas. A newly installed customs officer in Anahuac, a small community of colonists on Trinity Bay, where the last customs officer had caused violent resistance, had been fired upon by the colonists. A dispatch from

General Cós to the commanding officer at Anahuac fell into the hands of the Texans. The message urged the commander to be patient. Heavy reinforcements were on the way, the message said, adding, "In a very short time, the affairs of Texas will be settled."

William Barret Travis, a zealous leader of the War Dogs who had arrived in Texas in 1831, raised a force of about twenty-five men, acquired a small cannon, and decided to march on the Anahuac garrison before Cós's troops arrived. Travis's band of rebels reached Anahuac on June 29, 1835. At the garrison, they fired one shot from their cannon. The Mexican commander, realizing he was deep in rebel territory and not equipped to defend himself, promptly surrendered.

When word of the Mexican defeat at Anahuac reached General Cós, he ordered the arrest of Travis and a number of his men. Rumors circulated that the prisoners were to be court-martialed and shot. The colonists now rallied to support Travis and his War Party. While most of them agreed that Travis could be hotheaded and foolish, no one wanted him to be executed by a Mexican firing squad.

On September 1, 1835, Stephen Austin, tired and worn, arrived upon the scene following his release from a Mexico City jail. Austin had always preached that the colonists seek to understand and cooperate with the Mexican government. But now he believed that a peaceful solution was no longer possible. "War is our only recourse," Austin wrote to his fellow Texans. "There is no other remedy but to defend our rights, our country, and ourselves by force of arms."

The colonists listened to Austin and heeded his call to arms. Even those who had long been committed to cooperating with the Mexican government decided that such a policy was no longer possible. People everywhere began oiling their rifles and stockpiling ammunition. Towns and villages started forming militia companies. An uneasy peace prevailed. But most people realized that the tiniest spark could ignite open warfare.

That spark soon flared. Late in September 1835 Colonel Domingo de Ugartechea, the Mexican commander at San Antonio de Béxar, began a campaign to gather up weapons in the hands of the rebels. He sent a detachment of about 100 cavalrymen commanded by Lt. Francisco Castañeda seventy miles east to Gonzales to take a small cannon that had been given to the colonists several years earlier. Damaged and inexpertly repaired, the cannon had little firepower. But it was important to the colonists as a symbol, and they wouldn't think of surrendering it.

When the Mexican cavalrymen arrived at the west bank of the Río Guadalupe south of Gonzales, the colonists were on the east bank waiting for them, ready to fight. The colonists stalled the government forces and called for support. The growing ragtag band of volunteers, commanded by Col. John Henry Moore, one of Austin's original settlers, had its own flag, a big white rectangle of cotton cloth upon which had been painted a crude black cannon, a lone star above it, and the words COME AND TAKE IT.

The colonists were positioned so as to prevent the Mexican force from crossing the river. Castañeda decided to pull back his detachment to a position seven miles up the river. There they prepared to camp for the night and await further instructions from San Antonio. By this time, the rebel force numbered more than 150 volunteers. Under the cover of darkness, they set out in pursuit of the Mexicans. Their cannon went with them. They had mounted it on a primitive cart with wheels sliced from the trunk of a cottonwood tree.

Not long before dawn, the rebels located the Mexican camp. At daybreak, as a thick fog rose from the river, the rebel army advanced to within 350 yards of the Mexican camp, then fired the cannon. The startled Mexicans hurried into defensive positions.

Lieutenant Castañeda called for a conference. He met with Colonel Moore on horseback in the middle of a cornfield. Castañeda asked why the rebels were attacking his men. Moore responded with a lecture on the rights of the colonists. He also told the Mexican commander to surrender or fight.

Lieutenant Castañeda explained that his orders were to demand the cannon. Since he had been denied the weapon, he had to await further orders. Each commander then returned to his troops.

As Colonel Moore reached his own lines, he called out to his men, "Charge 'em boys, and give 'em hell!" A volley of rifle shots pierced the morning stillness and the cannon boomed. One Mexican soldier fell dead and several were wounded.

The date was October 2, 1835. The Texas Revolution had begun.

The Mexicans fled, abandoning much of their equipment and camping gear. They did not stop retreating until they were back in San Antonio de Béxar. The victorious rebels celebrated with a beef barbecue and all-night dancing.

Many rebel volunteers dressed in buckskins and armed themselves with muskets or Kentucky long rifles.

CHAPTER 4

REVOLUTION

Gonzales was only the beginning. After a week, a rebel contingent was on the march again. A Mexican military garrison at Mission La Bahía in Goliad, about ninety-five miles southeast of San Antonio, was their target. After a brief fight, the Mexican detachment of some forty men surrendered the strategic fort. As booty, the rebels claimed a big haul of rifles, powder, and shot.

Since the rebel victory at Gonzales, volunteers had been pouring into the town. They soon numbered more than 500 men. These volunteers had not signed up merely to support the cause of freedom. In exchange for their services, they had been promised land.

Volunteers who arrived with a working rifle and one hundred rounds of ammunition and stayed in the service until the end of the fighting were promised 1,280 acres. Six months of service earned a volunteer 640 acres; three months, 320 acres. Volunteers from twelve states and six foreign countries signed up to support the rebel cause.

The volunteers were for the most part completely untrained as soldiers. They had no organization and the barest of discipline. They also had no uniforms; some wore buckskin, some the clothes of planters and lawyers mixed with Mexican and Native American garments. Few wore boots; some had shoes; others, moccasins.

Stephen Austin was prevailed upon to come to Gonzales and command the volunteers. He did not especially want the job, but he was needed, so he accepted it.

The rebel army decided to move next on to San Antonio de Béxar, which General Cós had occupied with a force of more than a thousand men. When the volunteer army arrived on the outskirts of San Antonio de Béxar they paused. Although the rebels were bursting with confidence, thanks to their string of recent victories, they were not foolish enough to attack Cós and his far superior force. After the rebels surrounded Béxar, both sides settled down for a long siege. There were occasional exchanges of gunfire, but mainly both sides did nothing.

While the armed rebels fretted outside of San Antonio de Béxar and General Cós waited anxiously for them to make a move, delegates to the Consultation, the second convention the colonists formed to consider statehood, met at San Felipe de Austin. The chief issue they sought to decide was whether Texas was fighting for independence from Mexico or simply in defense of the Constitution of 1824, which Santa Anna had overturned when he came to power in 1833. The Peace Party called for support of the 1824 constitution, which was modeled to a large degree on the U.S. Constitution. They made it clear that while they opposed Santa Anna and his dictatorial rule, they did so as loyal Mexicans. The War Dogs, however, wanted Texas to declare its independence.

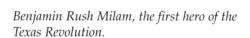

Benjamin Rush Milam, the first hero of the Texas Revolution.

Stephen Austin and many other delegates opposed such a move. Austin pointed out that such a course would make enemies out of those Mexicans who supported their cause and the many Tejanos who had already joined the rebellion. In the end the delegates formed their own provisional government but did not go so far as to declare independence. They voted to remain a part of Mexico so long as Mexico obeyed the provisions of the Federal Constitution of 1824.

Back in San Antonio, Edward Burleson, a land speculator who had come to Texas in 1830, had replaced Austin as the head of the rebel force. The men grumbled constantly about inactivity. Winter was approaching, and the nights were growing cold. Many men deserted for the comforts of home. They had not volunteered for a long war. They wanted action and quick victory. They then would receive the land they had been promised for volunteering.

One day a Mexican deserter and three Anglo-Americans managed to slip out of San Antonio. They reported that the morale of most of the Mexican soldiers was at a low point and their supplies were almost gone. Burleson decided to launch an attack. But then, believing that the Mexicans had gotten word of his plans, Burleson changed his mind. He decided to call off the assault and ordered the volunteers back to Gonzales.

But Burleson's decision was loudly challenged. Forty-seven-year-old Ben Milam, a Kentuckian and veteran of the War of 1812, and Francis W. Johnson, the second in command to Burleson, confronted the rebel leader in his tent and urged that the rebels take up the offensive. When Burleson would not commit himself, Milam decided to take matters into his own hands. Stepping outside the tent where the rebels waited, Milam took a rifle and used the butt to draw a line in the sand. He then called out, "Boys! Who will go with old Ben Milam into San Antonio?"

Hundreds of men shouted, "I will!"

Milam pointed to the line and said, "If you're going with me, get on this side." About 300 men stepped across the line to join Milam. Burleson now had no choice but to support the attack on San Antonio de Béxar.

Before dawn the next morning, December 5, Milam readied his men for the attack. A small detachment of sharpshooters opened fire, drawing the attention of Mexican gunners. At the same time, Milam sent the major part of his force streaming into the town. There they took cover in the houses of Tejanos.

Heavy gunfire kept the rebels pinned down. After two days, their situation seemed grim. Mexican cannonballs were destroying the adobe walls of the houses in which they had taken shelter.

The rebels had no choice but to advance. Using heavy crowbars, they began to punch big holes in the walls of the Tejano homes. They then moved grimly through the openings from one house into the next, until they finally took possession of two sturdily built stone houses on Military Plaza. One of these offered a panoramic view of the entire city. The Mexicans fought bitterly before giving it up. In the struggle, Ben Milam was struck by a bullet in the head and died instantly. School textbooks often hail him as the first hero of the Texas Revolution.

Francis Johnson replaced Milam as their leader, and the rebels renewed the attack. General Cós was forced to abandon San Antonio de Béxar, pulling his men back into the Alamo, the fortified compound of the abandoned Mission San Antonio de Valero.

From captured Mexican prisoners, the rebels learned that Cós was on the brink of defeat. Many of his best fighting men had deserted. His supplies of food and ammunition were almost gone. On the morning of December 9, 1835, Cós ordered the white flag of surrender to be flown. The bitter struggle was over. San Antonio and the Alamo were now in rebel hands.

Within the next twenty-four hours, peace terms were agreed upon. Cós was permitted to withdraw his troops back across the Rio Grande in exchange for a promise never again to take up arms against Texas and to do nothing to interfere with the restoration of the Constitution of 1824. The rebels had scored a major victory. And it had been achieved at a relatively low cost, for no more than three rebels had been killed, and twenty to thirty injured, in the fighting.

Hendrick Arnold played a key role as rebels ousted the Mexican Army from San Antonio and the Alamo.

Hendrick Arnold, a guide for Milam, was one of the volunteers who was hailed for having performed important service. Arnold's skills were so highly thought of that Milam's men refused to move until Arnold was there to lead them. At the time, no mention was made of the fact that Arnold was an African-American, perhaps because that fact was well known in Texas at the time.

With their victory, many rebels believed that they had won the war.

Sam Houston, chosen to lead the rebel army, emerged as a key figure in the Texas Revolution in 1833.

Santa Anna in Mexico City. As the revolution heated up, Houston emerged as one of its strongest leaders. He was chosen to command Texas's volunteers and later the regular army.

Houston was one of the few to realize that the Mexicans had been humiliated at Anahuac, Gonzales, Goliad, and San Antonio de Béxar. Those defeats were not going to go unpunished. Houston issued a call for volunteers. Time was short, he said. "The campaign cannot, in my opinion, be delayed with safety to the country much longer than the 20th of February, or the first day of March, at farthest," Houston declared.

Few people listened; few people cared. And few realized, as Houston did, that the biggest battles were to come.

Throughout the vast Texas territory, there was not one Mexican under arms. Texas was free. The rebel leaders looked forward to establishing statehood within the Mexican republic. The provisional government called for another convention, this one to be held at Washington-on-the-Brazos, to consider ways in which the state government might be made more effective. This consultation met on March 1, 1836, and is often called the Constitutional Convention.

Sam Houston, however, was wary of what the future might hold. Tall and strong, a powerful speaker and magnetic leader, Houston had earlier served as a member of the U.S. Congress from Tennessee and as governor of the state. He moved west to Arkansas and then to Nacogdoches, Texas, and had attended the San Felipe Convention of April 1, 1833, that had sent Austin to meet with

As a teenager, Sam Houston lived with a band of Cherokee Indians. In later life, he sometimes dressed in Cherokee clothing.

CHAPTER 5

"THE KEY TO TEXAS"

Long before General Cós had begun to have difficulties with the Texan volunteers at San Antonio de Béxar and the Alamo, Santa Anna had started to consider ways to put a quick end to the rebellion in Texas. Indeed, by the time Cós had delivered the Alamo over to the rebels and begun his sad march south, Santa Anna's plans were already being executed.

During the final months of 1835 Santa Anna had practically emptied the Mexican treasury to build an army of several thousand troops, most of them well-trained, well disciplined, loyal soldiers. The army assembled at Saltillo, and after adding General Cós's retreating army to the main force late in

Santa Anna assembled some 4,000 men in Mexico, then led the army on the long march north into Texas.

January, set out on the long march north.

As it made its way toward the Texas border, Santa Anna's army — some 5,000 to 6,000 men and twenty-one field cannons — stretched out for miles. First came the proud cavalry units, with Santa Anna and his entourage in front. The plodding lines of infantrymen followed, and then the army's supply train, made up of some 1,800 pack mules laden with food, and hundreds of wagons and carts, most pulled by oxen. Shuffling along at the rear was a throng of women and children. Besides providing companionship, the women cooked the army's meals.

The army reached the Rio Grande on February 12 and

began making preparations to cross into Texas. Santa Anna's strategy was simple. From the border, he planned to march north and east for 440 miles along the old Spanish highway — El Camino Real — all the way from the Rio Grande to the Sabine River, which formed Texas's eastern border with the United States. This meant he would have to go through San Antonio de Béxar. But that didn't worry Santa Anna. He didn't expect any serious opposition there.

Sam Houston had his own ideas on how to fight Santa Anna and his huge army. Houston wanted the rebels to develop a military force that would operate in small, independent groups, each capable of great speed and mobility. The rebels had the advantage of knowing the terrain, and their rifles were far more accurate and had greater range than the old muskets with which the Mexicans were equipped.

Houston believed the small bands of rebels should pounce on the Mexican troops, inflict what losses they could, then fall back, feint, and pounce again. It was a strategy the American colonists had used against the British army some sixty years earlier. It was also the strategy that the North Vietnamese and Vietcong would use against American forces in Southeast Asia in the late 1960s and early 1970s. It was guerrilla warfare. It would be possible to whittle down Santa Anna's army using such a strategy, stretching and eventually cutting his lines of supply, finally frustrating and defeating him. What the Americans

Mexican army officers dressed in dark blue uniforms and wore leather hats.

should not do, Houston believed, was meet the Mexican army head-on. Trying to defend the Alamo or any other such outpost would be a mistake.

Late in 1835, following the siege of San Antonio, a group of rebel leaders announced a foolish scheme to invade the Mexican port city of Matamoros, some 300 miles south of San Antonio on the Rio Grande. Houston opposed the idea. Even if the rebels were successful in gaining control of Matamoros, Houston foresaw nothing but trouble. Since it was hundreds of miles from supplies and reinforcements, the rebels would be hard-pressed to hold the city for any amount of time. Plainly speaking, the idea of attacking Matamoros was insane.

But neither Houston nor anyone else could persuade the rebels to abandon their plans. Thirty-two-year-old James Walker Fannin, a land speculator and slave trader from Georgia who had arrived in Texas in 1834 and served as a volunteer during the fighting at Béxar, was named to command the Matamoros operation. Once in charge, Fannin established headquarters at La Bahía, the small fortress he now called Fort Defiance, in the town of Goliad, and began recruiting volunteers. Although Houston was commander in chief of the military, he had no control over Fannin.

Houston also had to be upset by the situation at the Alamo. Col. James Clinton Neill, the rebel commander in San Antonio de Béxar, wrote to Henry Smith, governor of the provisional state, to complain that the garrison had been stripped of men and supplies for the Matamoros adventure. Neill said that 200 of his men had left to join Fannin at Goliad, leaving him only 104 men to defend San Antonio de Béxar and the Alamo. And when the men left, they had taken with them a mountain of supplies and food.

Neill's situation reinforced how Houston felt about the Alamo. He ordered Neill to abandon the Alamo and destroy the place. He then sent Jim Bowie, an old and trusted friend, to San Antonio de Béxar to make sure his orders would be carried out. On January 19 Bowie rode into San Antonio de Béxar

Colonel James Walker Fannin commanded rebel forces at Goliad.

with about thirty men who were to assist in the removal of the Alamo's guns and make whatever other preparations were necessary for the mission's destruction.

A man of great energy and daring, Bowie was no stranger in San Antonio de Béxar. He had first gone to Texas several years before, in 1828, made San Antonio de Béxar his home, become a Mexican citizen, and married Mária Veramendi, the daughter of a prominent Tejano family. As a prospector and speculator, Bowie had made a fortune in Texas land.

On his return, Bowie was warmly received by the Tejanos of San Antonio

Sent by Houston to destroy the Alamo's defenses, James Bowie decided instead to stay and fight.

and also heartily welcomed by Colonel Neill at the Alamo itself. The two military men discussed Houston's orders to abandon and destroy the Alamo — and decided to ignore them. Although Bowie realized that it would take a force of a thousand men to defend the mission against a Mexican onslaught, he concluded that the Alamo was vital to the defense of Texas.

In the days after his arrival, Bowie wrote to Governor Smith. "The salvation of Texas depends in a great measure in keeping Béxar out of the hands of the enemy," Bowie said. "It serves as the frontier picquet [sic] guard, and if it were in the possession of Santa Anna, there is no stronghold from which to repel him in his march toward the Sabine. Colonel Neill and myself have come to the solemn resolution that we will rather die in these ditches than give it up to the enemy."

Instead of preparing the Alamo for destruction as Houston had ordered, Bowie began to echo Neill's demands for food and supplies. One of Bowie's men, James Butler Bonham, organized a rally on January 26, 1836, at which the men passed a resolution calling for more supplies from the government. "We cannot be driven from the post of honor," the resolution said.

In mid-February Colonel Neill was forced to leave the Alamo on furlough to care for his sick family. That should have left Colonel Bowie in command. But by this time, William Barret Travis, also a colonel, had arrived upon the scene.

Travis was young — only twenty-six

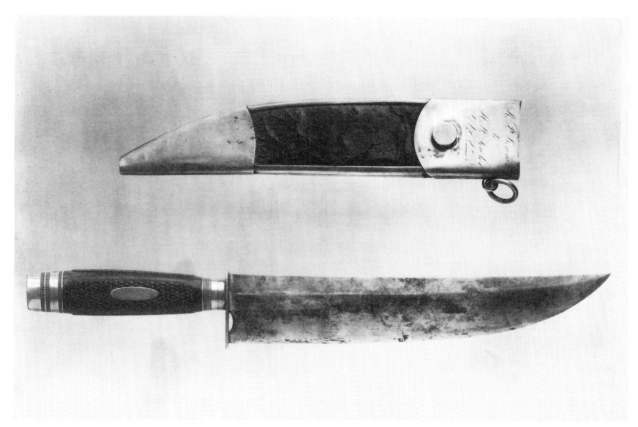

Famous knife designed by Bowie. Frontiersmen used it as both a tool and weapon.

— sensitive and moody, and very ambitious. It was Travis who led the march on the Mexican garrison at Anahuac during the previous summer and had accepted the surrender of the Mexican detachment. When the revolution began to heat up, Travis had asked Governor Smith to appoint him lieutenant colonel of the cavalry. But Travis had been able to attract only thirty of the volunteers he needed to serve in his cavalry legion.

When Governor Smith asked Travis to take his volunteers and ride off to San Antonio de Béxar to reinforce the Alamo, Travis was not pleased. He wrote to the governor, saying, "I am unwilling to risk my reputation . . . by going off into the enemy's country with such little means, so few men, and with them so badly equipped." Yet Travis did go, and within a week after his arrival, his attitude changed completely, and he became dedicated to the Alamo's defense. Writing the governor, Travis said, ". . . it is more important to occupy this Post than I imagined when I last saw you. It is the key to Texas."

Before Neill left the Alamo, he put Travis temporarily in command, since he was the senior regular army officer. But it was not a popular choice among the volunteers, who preferred Bowie.

It was not a popular choice with Bowie, either. While he had always gotten along well with Travis, Bowie did not like the idea of of taking orders from the young and self-important newcomer.

Travis realized he was in an awkward situation. To ease the pressure, he ordered the volunteers to hold an election to choose their commanding officer. The men voted for Bowie.

The result was that the Alamo command was now divided. The volunteers had Bowie, but Travis still commanded his cavalry unit and the regular army troops. All major decisions had to be made and signed by both men. It was a troublesome situation.

As the rebel leaders bickered at the Alamo, Santa Anna and his huge army, their cannon, pack mules, and hundreds of wheeled carts and wagons were crossing the Rio Grande into Texas. At the border, Santa Anna had met up with General Cós and his nearly one thousand soldiers who were retreating into Mexico. They were the ragged remnants of a Mexican force that the rebels had ousted from San Antonio de Béxar in December. In exchange for their freedom, Cós had promised the rebel leaders that his men would not fight again. Santa Anna angrily told Cós to forget what he had promised, turn his detachment around, and march with him into Texas. Although Cós's men had already marched thousands of miles, and many were dying of hunger and thirst, Cós had no choice but to obey orders. He and his men joined forces with Santa Anna.

At the beginning of the third week in February, a rebel spy arrived in San Antonio to reveal that he personally witnessed the Mexican army crossing the river. Travis, who believed that Santa Anna would never attempt to cross the plains to San Antonio during the winter, decided that the man must be mistaken or was not telling the truth. He and his officers chose to ignore the report. But already, Santa Anna's army was encamped near the Río Honda, with the Alamo less than fifty miles away.

CHAPTER 6

VICTORY OR DEATH

"You can plainly see that the Alamo never was built by military people as a fortress," Green B. Jameson wrote to Sam Houston on January 18, 1836. Jameson was a twenty-nine-year-old Kentuckian who had established a law practice in San Felipe de Austin but left it behind to join the volunteers. While he was schooled as a lawyer, he had natural talents as a military engineer. When the decision was made to defend the Alamo, Jameson took the job of making it secure.

It was no easy task. The Alamo had been founded in 1718 by Spanish priests as the Mission San Antonio de Valero. It was later moved from the west bank to the east bank of the San Antonio River.

Construction of what was later to be known as the Long Barracks, which contained living quarters and a dining room, was completed in 1744. And in 1756 construction began on the mission church that now occupies the site. Partly because of a series of epidemics, the Spanish closed the mission in 1793 and distributed the farmlands among the mission Indians.

Mexican cavalry troops took over the site in 1821. The cavalry unit came from Álamo de Parras in Coahuila, Mexico. As a result, the former mission became known as "Pueblo del Alamo" or, simply, the Alamo.

At the time Bowie, Travis, and their rebel troops began occupying the Alamo, the mission-church stood at one corner of the compound. The church's walls were still standing but the roof had collapsed. A platform of heavy timbers for three cannon had been built at one end of the church by General Cós in his unsuccessful defense of the Alamo the previous December. A dirt ramp leading to the platform filled much of the church's interior.

The thick walls of cut stone provided protection for those within. But there were no slits in the walls through which the men could aim their guns. And although General Cós had left behind

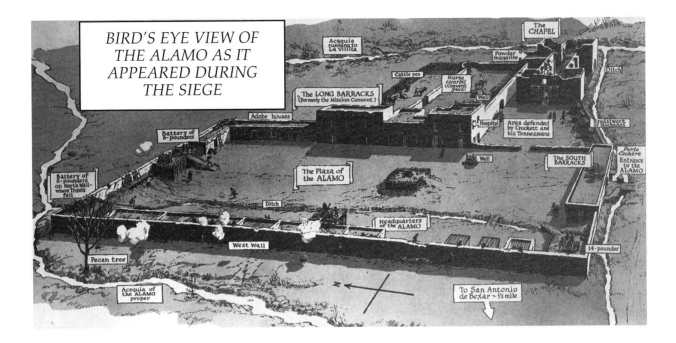

BIRD'S EYE VIEW OF THE ALAMO AS IT APPEARED DURING THE SIEGE

twenty-one cannons, there were no platforms on which the cannons could be placed to fire over the walls.

Despite the problems, Jameson was enthusiastic about converting the Alamo into a makeshift fortress. He was helped by Capt. Almeron Dickinson, a twenty-six-year-old blacksmith from Tennessee who had settled in Gonzales. After the Alamo had been taken over by the rebels, Dickinson brought his fifteen-year-old wife, Susannah, and their infant daughter, Angelina, to San Antonio de Béxar to live.

Jameson and Dickinson had timber-and-earthen platforms built behind the stone walls and placed cannons atop them. They positioned the biggest of the cannons, which were capable of launching an eighteen-pound ball, at the southwest corner of the compound. Jameson used upright logs to fill gaps in the wall, particularly a large opening between the church and the Low Barracks. And to increase the water supply, he had an old well reopened.

Despite their ingenuity and hard work, the two men could not overcome the problem of the Alamo's size. Covering about three acres, almost the size of a city block, the compound was simply too large to be adequately defended by a force of something less than 200 men.

After the rebels had overcome the Mexican soldiers defending San Antonio de Béxar in December, nearly all of them had returned to their homes. The men who stayed were mostly mercenaries, that is, hired guns. Only a handful had been in Texas for as long as six years. They included lawyers, physicians, clerks, blacksmiths, and brickmasons. There were no professional soldiers among them.

Aside from Jim Bowie, the most

A backwoods legend and one-time Tennessee Congressman, Davy Crockett came to be looked upon as the most famous of the Alamo defenders.

famous of the Alamo defenders was frontiersman Davy Crockett. He arrived at the Alamo on February 8, leading a band of a dozen sharpshooters that he called his "Tennessee Mountain Volunteers." Nearly fifty years old at the time, Crockett was a legendary figure, and his arrival triggered a noisy celebration.

Noted as a soldier, scout, hunter, and expert rifleman, Crockett had used his reputation to launch a political career. Famous, too, as a storyteller, he often made fun of his lack of education. Correct spelling, he said, was something "contrary to nature" and grammar "nothing at all." Crockett had served three terms in Congress but was defeat-

ed for a fourth. Following his loss, he set out for Texas, where he hoped he might resume his political career and become rich as a land agent.

Crockett's volunteers included Daniel W. Cloud and Peter James Bailey, both recent law school graduates. After leaving their homes in Kentucky, they had traveled to Illinois, Missouri, Arkansas, and Louisiana in their search for a community where they could settle down and set up practice. Each state was a disappointment to them and they kept moving on. Texas now loomed as their land of opportunity.

Cloud seemed to be speaking for many of the rebels when he wrote, "Ever since Texas has unfurled the banner of Freedom, and commenced a Warfare of liberty or death, our hearts have been enlisted in her behalf. . . . If we succeed, the Country is ours. It is immense in extent and fertile in its soil, and will amply reward all our toil. If we fail, death in the cause of Liberty and humanity is not a cause for shuddering. . . ."

A number of Tejanos also volunteered to defend the Alamo. Their vision of freedom was not something new. It could be traced to a time long before Santa Anna and his dictatorial policies. During the period in which Spain ruled Mexico, Mexican Texans were tormented by Spanish governors who were Centralists, too, holding views similar to Santa Anna's. The present conflict was merely a continuation of their struggle for self-determination.

The Tejano volunteers were commanded by twenty-nine-year-old Juan

In the movie "The Alamo," released in 1960, Crockett was portrayed by Hollywood superstar John Wayne (center).

N. Seguín, a Texas-born Mexican who had organized some of the Tejano ranchers along the San Antonio River into a cavalry unit. His father, Erasmo Seguín, had served as *alcalde*, or mayor, of San Antonio de Béxar. In 1821, the elder Seguín was one of the officials who had greeted Stephen Austin on his first visit to Texas. Juan Seguín strongly opposed Santa Anna. His hope was that one day Texas would be an independent republic, free of Mexico, and free of the United States as well.

As the federalist rebels readied for the

Juan Seguín organized the Tejano unit that fought in defense of Alamo. This oil portrait was painted in 1838.

battle to come, the Mexican army was moving steadily north. Travis and the men of the Alamo heard one rumor after another saying that the Mexicans were on the way. But Travis had no faith in these reports.

On February 21 the Mexican army reached the banks of the Medina River. San Antonio was only twenty-five miles to the north.

The next day, February 22, George Washington's birthday, was a day of celebrating for the Anglo-Americans. Almost the entire garrison of the Alamo and well over a thousand townspeople joined together for a fiesta, with much food, dancing, and drink. The celebrating continued until well after midnight.

Early the next morning, Travis and many of the men of the Alamo were awakened by the sound of oxcarts lumbering out of town. Hundreds of residents had emptied their homes and were fleeing. Those who couldn't ride, walked.

Travis wanted to find out what was happening. He ordered the arrest of a handful of townspeople. When he questioned them, Travis learned nothing. Finally, a Tejano who was friendly to the rebels revealed that during the night a messenger from Santa Anna brought word to the townspeople that his army was advancing on San Antonio de Béxar and planned to attack the next day. The people were told to evacuate.

Travis sent two men to investigate. They galloped out to a hill about a mile and a half from town. From the top, they looked down upon a scene that drew gasps from them both — several hundred Mexican cavalrymen lined up in battle formation. The unit's commanding officer rode up and down the line, waving his sword. The Mexicans had arrived; there could be no doubt about it. The two men raced back to the Alamo to warn Travis.

Not long after, a lookout in the bell tower of San Antonio's San Fernando Church began ringing the church bell in alarm. The Anglo-Americans who lived in San Antonio de Béxar understood what the ringing meant and began hurrying toward the Alamo.

Capt. Almeron Dickinson left his post and galloped to the house where his wife and infant daughter were staying. "The Mexicans are upon us!" he shouted. "Give me the baby and jump up behind me!" Then the family galloped to the Alamo.

A Mexican woman, as she watched the Anglo-Americans fleeing across the narrow bridge from the town to the Alamo, shook her head sadly and said, "Poor fellows, you will all be killed."

When the gates for the Alamo were closed and barred there were about 150 fighting men inside. There were also some thirty to forty civilians crowded into the old mission, mostly women and children. They included several black slaves brought as servants by Travis and other officers.

By midafternoon, the Mexican cavalry had filed into San Antonio de Béxar, occupying the town without firing a shot. Inside the Alamo, Travis began to

The barrel of the famous 18-pound cannon is now displayed in the courtyard of the Alamo complex.

prepare for battle, conferring with his officers and assigning his men to their positions. Travis deployed Davy Crockett and his men along the wall of tree trunks that Jameson had erected between the church and the Low Barracks. It was a weak point in the Alamo defense, and Travis knew it would be stronger with Crockett and his men behind it.

Late in the afternoon, rebel lookouts watched as the Mexicans hoisted a great red banner in the bell tower of the San Fernando Church. Travis and his men knew exactly what it meant. The flag signaled no mercy; Santa Anna would take no prisoners.

Defending the Alamo had become a matter of victory or death.

Travis had an immediate response. He ordered the eighteen-pound cannon to be fired. No particular target was singled out. Travis simply meant the firing to be a bold act of defiance.

Bowie and many others in the Alamo were shocked by what Travis had done.

They had hoped to be able to negotiate with Santa Anna. The booming cannon shot committed the Alamo's defenders to fighting to the end. To Bowie and others within the Alamo's walls, this seemed insane, considering the size of the Mexican army as compared with their own tiny garrison.

Santa Anna answered Travis's cannon shot by ordering his artillery to fire several grenades into the Alamo compound. The firing stopped when a lone rider emerged from the Alamo bearing a white flag of peace. The rider was Green Jameson, the Alamo's chief military engineer. He carried a message that had been hastily scribbled by Bowie asking whether the Mexicans wished to negotiate.

Santa Anna refused to answer the message himself; he would not seek to come to terms with "rebellious foreigners," he said. Jameson returned to the Alamo with a reply from an officer on Santa Anna's staff. The only terms were unconditional surrender, the reply said.

CHAPTER 7

UNDER SIEGE

Travis had fired the cannon without consulting Bowie. Bowie had tried to negotiate with Santa Anna without Travis's consent. Who was in charge? There was obviously friction between the sensitive, thin-skinned Travis and the popular, independent Bowie.

Their differences might have led to a heated dispute over command of the Alamo, but Bowie fell ill. His illness has been described as "a disease of a peculiar nature." It might have been tuberculosis, pneumonia, diptheria, or typhoid fever. Whatever it was, Bowie collapsed completely, falling onto his cot. That left the Alamo in the command of one man — Travis.

During Travis's first night in charge, the Mexicans moved artillery into position — two cast-iron cannons, each weighing two tons and capable of hurling a nine-pound iron sphere a distance of a quarter of a mile. Early in the afternoon, the pounding began. Shot rained down onto the Alamo, tearing into buildings and walls. The rebels' eighteen-pounder was hit and knocked off its mount.

Santa Anna's artillerymen also blasted away with howitzers, short-barreled guns that fire a hollow metal sphere filled with powder and fitted with a fuse cut to a length appropriate for the distance the shell was to travel. The fuse was ignited before the shell was inserted into the gun. Howitzer shells were lobbed over the Alamo walls and timed to explode inside.

Despite the bombardment, there were no casualties inside the garrison. Occasionally the rebels answered back with their own artillery blasts, but most of the time they thought it wiser to conserve powder and shot, which were in short supply.

During periods of calm, Travis sat down with pen and paper and wrote appeals for help. One of his letters went to Sam Houston. "Do hasten to aid me as rapidly as possible," Travis wrote, "as from the superior number of the enemy,

THE TRAVIS LETTER FROM THE ALAMO

Commandancy of the Alamo --
Bejar, Feby, 24th, 1836

To the People of Texas and All Americans --

Fellow Citizens & compatriots --

    I am besieged, by a thousand or more Mexicans under Santa Anna -- I have sustained a continual Bombardment & cannonade for 24 hours and have not lost a man -- The enemy has demanded a surrender at discretion, otherwise, the garrison are to be put to the sword, if the fort is taken -- I have answered the demand with a cannon shot, & our flag still waves proudly from the walls -- **I shall never surrender or retreat** Then, I call on you in the name of Liberty, of patriotism & everything dear to the American character, to come to our aid, with all dispatch -- The enemy is receiving reinforcements daily & will no doubt increase to three or four thousand in four or five days. If this call is neglected, I am determined to sustain myself as long as possible & die like a soldier who never forgets what is due to his own honor & that of this country --VICTORY OR DEATH.

William Barret Travis
Lt. Col. comdt.

This letter of appeal from Travis helped to make him a hero. In it, he declared, "I shall never surrender or retreat."

it will be impossible for us to keep them out much longer. If they overpower us, we fall a sacrifice at the shrine of our country, and we hope posterity and our country will do our memory justice. Give me help, oh my Country!"

Travis chose Captain Juan Seguín to carry this message. Borrowing Jim Bowie's horse, Seguín managed to outwit and outride the Mexican sentinels who challenged him and speed toward Gonzales.

Travis's many appeals never brought him the aid he sought. In response to one of his messages to Col. James Fannin at Goliad, Fannin had set out on February 28 for the Alamo with a relief expedition of several hundred men. But after a supply wagon broke down and other mishaps occurred, Fannin decided to abandon the mission and return to Goliad.

The only unit to respond to Travis's cries for help was a small militia company that had been formed by George Kimbell, a New York hatter who had settled in Gonzales. Kimbell and thirty-two other volunteers arrived at the Alamo early on the morning of February 29. Unfortunately, they brought no food or ammunition with them, but able defenders now numbered 183.

By this time, Santa Anna's troops had surrounded the Alamo. But they kept

During the siege, Santa Anna made his headquarters on San Antonio's main plaza, in the low building just to the left of the Plaza House.

back beyond 200 yards, for the range of the rebel Kentucky long rifles was deadly accurate to that distance.

Santa Anna's army grew by the hour as more and more troops arrived. The Mexicans built new earthworks to protect their artillery, which now fired at the Alamo from every point of the compass. Once in a while, rebel sharpshooters would spot a mounted figure they thought to be Santa Anna far in the distance, but they were not able to bring him down.

Throughout the siege, the rebels never stopped watching and waiting — and working. They repaired damaged earthworks and reset guns toppled from their mounts by artillery fire. They dug trenches in the plaza and sneaked out several times to set fire to nearby wooden shacks close to the Alamo that could be used to shelter Mexican soldiers. When there was a lull in the artillery fire, they slept or ate. Occasionally a unit of Mexicans would charge, and the rebels would force them back with blistering rifle fire, leaving dozens of Mexicans dead or wounded.

Each morning, the rebels could see that the Mexican artillery pieces had been moved a bit closer. And each day, they could see more and more Mexican soldiers.

During the early days of the siege, rumors raced through the Alamo that Colonel Fannin and his troops were on the way. And when George Kimbell and his militiamen arrived, demonstrating that the Mexican lines were not hard to penetrate, the rebels' hopes for relief

"Dawn at the Alamo" by Henry McArdle depicts the siege.

were bolstered. If Kimbell and his thirty-two men, armed only with rifles, could make it through, surely Fannin and his force of more than 400 could. After all, Fannin had artillery. Every day Travis and his men looked out toward the

horizon for some sign of Fannin and his troops.

On February 27, Travis sent James Bonham to Goliad, 100 miles southeast of the Alamo, to appeal to Fannin for help. When Bonham arrived, he found Fannin in a grim mood and not eager to leave the safety of his fort. He sent Bonham back to the Alamo with several excuses explaining why he could not send reinforcements. Bonham made it back on March 3 and gave the bad news to Travis. Fannin's troops were not coming. Travis took the news in stride. He would not permit himself to become discouraged.

In total, Travis sent sixteen messages from the Alamo carrying his desperate requests for help. In his final letter of appeal, sent to Gonzales, Travis said, "At least two hundred shells have fallen inside of our works without having injured a single man; indeed, we have been so fortunate as not to lose a man from any cause, and we have killed many of the enemy. The spirits of my men are still high."

On Friday morning, March 4, the rebel riflemen noticed that the Mexicans had moved their artillery even closer. It was now only about 250 yards away. All day long the guns bombarded the Alamo. The next day brought more of the same. The Alamo walls were beginning to fall to pieces and in some places the defenders were unable to repair them.

In the distance, beyond the range of their rifles, the rebels could see Mexican soldiers making ladders. They could be meant for only one purpose: to scale the Alamo's crumbling walls.

Late in the afternoon of March 5, there was a letup in the Mexican bombardment. Travis took advantage of the pause to call his men together in the open plaza, then made a short speech outlining the realities of the situation. They could fight, escape, or surrender. Travis said that he had made up his mind to stay and die. He urged his men to remain with him but added he would not force anyone to do so.

It was at this point that Travis is said to have taken his sword and drawn a line in the sand, and then invited those who wished to stay with him to cross it. One man stepped forward, then another, and then others in small clusters. Jim Bowie, lying helpless on his cot, is supposed to have said, "I can't make it across the line; will some of you give me a hand?" Four men stepped forward, each took a corner of Bowie's cot, and carried him across.

Only one man, Louis "Moses" Rose, chose not to cross. An older man who had fought with Napoleon, Rose decided it would be better to live and fight another day. He escaped from the Alamo that night. Every other man stayed.

CHAPTER 8

STORMING THE ALAMO

At the same time the rebels were considering their fate, Santa Anna was making plans for what he hoped would be a final assault upon the Alamo. His plan was to divide his infantrymen into four columns, each with about 800 men. Two columns would attack the northeast and northwest corners; another would take the east wall, while the fourth would target upon the line of tree trunks between the church and the Low Barracks, the Alamo's weakest point. Santa Anna deployed the Mexican cavalry behind the infantry with orders to see to it that no rebels escaped and no Mexicans deserted. He personally commanded his fifth column of reserves.

The attack began at 5 o'clock on the morning of Sunday, March 6. It came as no surprise to the men within the Alamo. The quiet of the morning was broken by the blaring of a bugle that could be heard by the rebels as well as the Mexican infantry. Other buglers repeated the call. As the sound of the bugles died, hundreds of Mexican infantrymen cheered and rushed to cross the 200 to 300 yards that separated them from the Alamo's walls.

Capt. John Baugh, a Virginian and the second in command to Travis, was on the wall. He heard the bugles and the cries and raced for Travis's room, crying, "Colonel Travis, the Mexicans are coming!" Travis jumped out of bed, grabbed his sword and a double-barreled shotgun, and raced to the north wall.

The oncoming Mexicans were met with a storm of rebel rifle and cannon fire. Some of the men had placed three or four loaded rifles at their posts and fired them one after another before having to pause and reload.

The Mexican column attacking from the east was slowed almost to a stop by the murderous cannon fire from the mission church. Besides cannonballs, the rebels loaded their artillery pieces with clusters of musket balls and chopped up horseshoes, door hinges, nails, and other pieces of scrap iron. Grapeshot, as it is

Travis was one of the first to fall during the Mexican army's final assault.

called, is almost as deadly as modern-day machine gun fire.

Davy Crockett's sharpshooters managed to turn back the Mexicans attacking the south wall. On the north side, cannon fire ripped into the Mexican column, causing heavy losses. A few Mexicans managed to reach the wall, however. Col. Francisco Duqué, who commanded the column attacking from the north, went down with a shattered leg. His own men trampled over his body.

From his vantage point at the north wall, Travis emptied his shotgun into the ranks of the Mexicans below. Then, suddenly, he tumbled backward, a bullet in his forehead. He sat up for a moment — still clutching his sword — looked about, then died. Travis was one of the first defenders to be killed.

For a time it seemed as if the deadly rebel fire from atop the walls had turned back the attack. But it was only a momentary pause. Shouting with fury and urgency, the Mexican officers whipped their men forward a second time. Again, the blistering rebel fire blunted the assault. But the brave Mexicans could not be stopped. They came a third time, many of them cheering and yelling as they advanced.

The column of troops advancing toward the east wall was stopped again, but instead of falling back, the men drifted to the right, joining the column on the north. At the same time, the column on the northwest veered in the other direc-

Furious final moments of the siege were depicted by E. Percy Moran in his painting "Battle of the Alamo."

tion, to the left, and also combined with the north column. The result was a surging throng of men, all pressing toward the Alamo's north wall.

When the first troops finally reached the wall, they milled about in a confused mass. The ladders they needed to scale the walls were nowhere to be seen. The ladder carriers had either been shot or had fled.

Watching at some distance to the rear, Santa Anna believed his men were being routed. Filled with alarm, he ordered his reserve unit into action. The 400 officers and men who made up the reserves rushed forward, cheering and firing their rifles as they went. Some of their bullets found the shoulders and backs of the men ahead of them.

Now a critical turning point occurred. The swarming Mexican troops at the foot of the north wall reached an earthwork supported by bare timbers and wooden braces that had been built by Jameson in front of a damaged section of wall to strengthen it. Despite rebel fire pouring down on them from above, Mexican troops started scrambling up the sides of earthwork, using it as a ladder. Some troops fell away, dead or wounded, but there were others to take their places. Gen. Juan Amador reached the top, his men beside him, and then it was over the wall. Now the Mexicans were inside the Alamo.

At the same time, another mass of attackers were charging the northwest side of the Alamo. There was no earth-

Death is said to have come to Jim Bowie as he lay on his sickbed.

work there but at several points the rebels had punched holes in the wall, through which they could aim and fire their guns. The Mexicans squeezed through the holes. A few scaling ladders were brought up, and Mexican troops climbed the wall and jumped down into the plaza below. The first men inside opened the north gate from within and more soldiers streamed in.

Mexican troops also managed to scale the wall at the Alamo's southwest corner, climbing up the sides to capture the rebels' eighteen-pound cannon. The rebels fought frantically, using knives, bayonets, and their rifles as clubs, but the Mexicans kept coming.

Mexican troops were now pouring into the Alamo at three points — over the north wall, through the gate at the northwest corner, and at the southwest corner. The rebels met the Mexicans in the Alamo's open plaza. After several minutes of savage hand-to-hand fighting, the rebels retreated to the the Low Barracks, the many small buildings that fringed the plaza, and the crumbling chapel. There they made their last stand.

One by one, the Mexicans blasted the rooms of the Low Barracks with cannonballs, then used pistols, bayonets, and knives to push from room to room. Before long, the building was in Mexican hands and every rebel lay dead.

In his room in the Low Barracks, the Mexican soldiers stormed in to find Jim Bowie, defenseless on his bed. According to an account given by Bowie's horror-stricken sister-in-law, they "tossed Bowie's body on their bayonets until his blood covered their clothes and dyed them red." However, there are various accounts of Bowie's death that conflict with the account given by his sister-in-law.

CHAPTER 9

THE FALL OF THE ALAMO

Santa Anna had ordered that only women be spared, and that order was carried out. But the Mexican soldiers killed every man they could find. To be sure nobody escaped, they poked their bayonets into corpses or fired into them. They killed the sick and wounded in the hospital. In their frenzy, they even killed a stray cat.

The last building to fall to the Mexicans was the mission church. There Susannah Dickinson waited in the darkness for the end, holding Angelina close. The Mexican soldiers battered down the door and stormed inside. One of the rebels grabbed a torch

Susannah Dickinson in middle age. She was in her early 20's at the time of the fall of the Alamo.

and dashed toward a room at the side of the chapel where several hundred pounds of gunpowder had been stored, hoping to explode it. The soldiers shot him before he could ignite the powder.

A Mexican officer appeared in the doorway of Susannah Dickinson's room. "Is Mrs. Dickinson here?" the officer asked.

Too frightened to answer, Dickinson shrank into the shadows in the far corner of the room. "Is Mrs. Dickinson here?" the officer asked again. "Speak out, for it is a matter of life or death."

When Dickinson did step forward, several soldiers leaped to seize her. One shot her

According to one account, Davy Crockett died "fighting like a wild beast."

The battle was drawing to an end. The last defenders were being hunted down in the Alamo's dark rooms.

Nearly every man present died in the defense of the Alamo. Many people were unsure exactly what these men had died for. They did not know that fifty-nine delegates to a Texas Constitutional Convention had met at the village of Washington-on-the-Brazos beginning on March 1 and formed a new government. Having abandoned the hope of becoming a state with the federation of Mexico, the delegates had declared their independence as a free and sovereign nation on March 2, 1836.

On Sunday, March 6, the delegates crowded into the meeting room to listen to the reading of a message from Colonel Travis at the Alamo, in which he appealed for reinforcements, ammunition, and provisions. The delegates were deeply moved by Travis's words. Some wanted to rush to his rescue. But by that time, Travis was already dead, and the Alamo was in Mexican hands.

The Mexican dead and wounded amounted to more than 600, about one-sixth of the attacking force. The number

in the right calf, and she fell bleeding. The officer shouted at the men, telling them to back off, no doubt saving her life. The terrified young woman was later treated by a Mexican surgeon and allowed to leave the Alamo with her daughter.

Four or five rebels tried to escape from the Alamo, hurtling themselves over the walls. But by this time, the sun was up and the men were quickly seized by Mexican cavalrymen. All were slain by Mexicans wielding knives or bayonets.

An artist's conception of the Mexican army's final assault.

of dead may have been as many as two or three times that amount. No one knows the true number, for Santa Anna ordered the Mexican bodies to be buried as quickly as possible after the battle had ended.

Of the Alamo, Santa Anna said, "Much blood has been shed; but the battle is over; it was but a small affair."

But in truth, the Alamo was anything but "a small affair" to the Mexican army, costing many more lives than could ever be justified. Gen. Vicente Filisola, Santa Anna's second in command, was very critical of Santa Anna's tactics. Filisola questioned the need for the Mexican

forces, with their vast numerical superiority, to have launched an all-out assault upon the Alamo. Filisola pointed out that the Mexican army could simply have surrounded the Alamo and starved the rebels into submission, or they could have persuaded them to surrender — if surrender had been offered as a choice.

Despite the heavy loss of life, 90 percent of the full Mexican army was still intact and its march across Texas was scarcely slowed.

Late in the day of his Alamo conquest, Santa Anna had ordered the bodies of Mexican soldiers to be loaded into

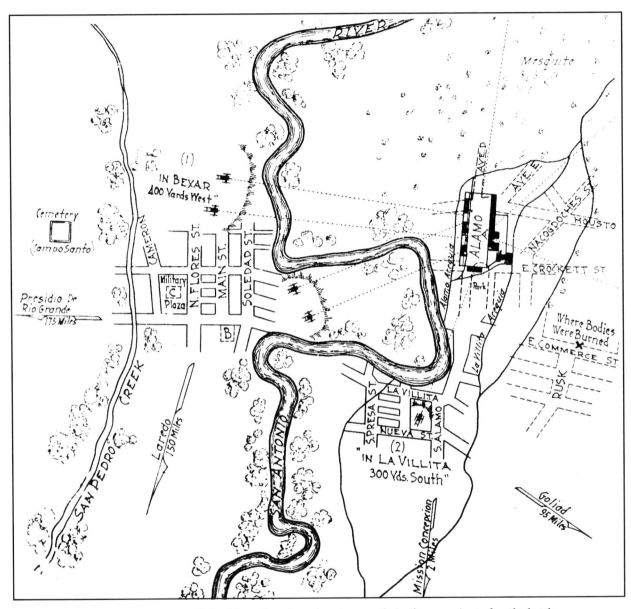

A map of San Antonio de Béxar and the Alamo based on drawings made in the years just after the battle.

oxcarts and hauled to a nearby cemetery for burial. For the fallen rebels, there would be no final resting place. Santa Anna sent soldiers into neighboring forests to collect wood and dry branches. The wood was used to build a giant pyre: layers of bodies between layers of wood. Not long before dusk on the afternoon of March 6, the pyre was lighted.

Early in 1837, Capt. Juan Seguín, who was then stationed at San Antonio de Béxar, gathered some of the ashes and bone that remained where the base of the pyre had been and had them placed in a coffin. The names of Travis, Bowie, and Crockett were engraved on the coffin lid. On February 25, 1837, the coffin was buried in a peach orchard not far from the Alamo.

News of the fall of the Alamo and the bravery of the defenders united Texans like no event before or since. It triggered a deep rage that made them want to strike back at Santa Anna, whom they branded a tyrant and a butcher. "Remember the Alamo!" became their battle cry.

CHAPTER 10

SURVIVORS AND VICTIMS

A handful of men, women, and children lived through the siege of the Alamo. Susannah Dickinson and her infant daughter, Angelina, who became known as "The Babe of the Alamo," were the most famous of the survivors. Both led troubled lives in the years that followed the Alamo's fall. Mrs. Dickinson married and divorced several times before settling down in central Texas in the cabinet-making business with her fifth husband. She outlived her daughter, who married at sixteen, had several children, and died as she was approaching her mid-thirties.

Juan Seguín, an early opponent of Santa Anna and leader of the Tejano unit that defended the Alamo, had served as one of Travis's messengers and was on his way back to the Alamo when he learned the fortress had fallen. Seguín later fought bravely in Sam Houston's army at the Battle of San Jacinto. He went on to be elected to the Senate of the Republic of Texas and twice won election as mayor of San Antonio. Seguín,

Susannah Dickinson's daughter, Angelina, "The Babe of the Alamo."

In the years following the battle of the Alamo, Juan Seguín was branded a traitor and forced to flee to Mexico. He was jailed in Laredo by Santa Anna.

Texas, about thirty-five miles east of San Antonio, was named in his honor in 1839.

But Seguín was later painted as a traitor, a supporter of Mexicans who were planning to invade and retake Texas, and compelled to flee to Mexico. There he was confronted by Santa Anna, who forced Seguín to join a Mexican force that attacked Texas during the war between Mexico and the United States (1846–1848). Seguín died in 1890.

Other Tejanos who fought with the rebels at the Alamo included Juan Abamillo, Juan Antonio Badtillo, Carlos Espalier, José Gregorio Esparza, Antonio Fuentes, Brigido Guerrero, Toribio Losoya, Andres Nava, and Damacio Ximenes.

Gregorio Esparza was killed while manning a cannon for the rebels. After the battle, his widow, Anna, and her small children — Enrique, Francisco, Manuel, and Maria de Jesus — were discovered hovering near their father's body.

I leave this rule, for others when I am dead
Be always sure, you are right, then go, a head

David Crockett

According to legend, Davy Crockett was one of the first to die fighting in the Alamo. But recent evidence indicates he may have been taken prisoner and executed.
(Collection of The New-York Historical Society)

Many years later, Enrique Esparza, who was under ten years old at the time of the siege, said that he would have fought had he been given a chance. But guns were scarce and handed out only to those who were skilled in their use. In addition, his parents were not anxious for him to fight.

"Shots were fired fast. Bullets were thick," Enrique Esparza once told the *San Antonio Daily Express.* "Both men and women fell within the walls. Even children died there." He described the days "as long and filled with terror.

"Crockett seemed to be the leading spirit. He was everywhere. Travis was in command, but he depended more upon the judgement of Crockett . . . than his own."

Gregorio Esparza and his young son, Enrique, at a cannon during the Alamo battle.

Hand-carved mural by Jesse Garcia at Esparza Elementary School depicts Gregorio Esparza and his family during the Alamo siege.

Several of the survivors were, like Juan Seguín, messengers. Another was John W. Smith, who carried one of Travis's last appeals for help to the Constitutional Convention held at Washington-on-the-Brazos. After the fall of the Alamo, Smith entered politics and was elected mayor of San Antonio three times.

Other survivors included Gertrudis Navarro, fifteen, and her sister Juana Navarro de Alsbury, the adopted sisters of Jim Bowie's wife, and Juana's eighteen-month-old son, Alijo Perez, Jr. They were found amidst the ruins during the final stages of battle and taken to the chapel.

Travis's twenty-three-year-old black slave, known only as Joe, also managed to survive the ordeal and was spared. Joe was treated with respect for a time but eventually was put to work as a slave again, planting cotton for a dollar a day. He escaped, was captured, and made to return to a life of servitude.

Louis "Moses" Rose was another survivor who endured a harsh life. It was Rose who rejected Travis's invitation to fight to the end and fled from the Alamo before the real fighting began. Rose settled in Nacogdoches, where he became known as a deserter and was treated with contempt as a result. When an attempt on Rose's life was made by a drunken man, the townspeople shrugged. No charges were filed against the assailant.

For others, survival was a death warrant. After the battle, half a dozen rebels, including a fourteen-year-old boy, were found hiding in a back room of the chapel. When soldiers rushed into the room, intent upon shooting or bayoneting them, a general named Manuel Fernandez Castrillón happened to be present and called them off.

Castrillón brought his captives to Santa Anna, who had entered the mission to inspect the scene. Castrillón suggested that a show of mercy might be in order for what he described as "six brave prisoners of war."

One of the captives was Davy Crockett. To Santa Anna, Crockett and the other prisoners were smugglers, slave traders, and selfish mercenaries. "I do not want to see these men living," Santa Anna declared. "Shoot them!"

With that, several soldiers, swords in hand, pounced upon the poor captives and cut them down. José Enrique de la Peña, one of Santa Anna's brightest officers, was a witness to the slaughter. He later wrote, "I confess that the very memory of it makes me tremble and that

Señora Candelaria, believed by many to have been an Alamo survivor, spun tales of Bowie, Crockett, and other Alamo defenders. Here she poses with her dog.

my ear can still hear the penetrating, doleful sound of the victims."

In the decades that followed the fall of the Alamo, a legend grew that Crockett had gone down fighting, flailing away at the Mexican soldiers swarming about him with the butt of his trusted rifle "Ole Betsy." It seems as if no one wanted to remember that Crockett had been captured and executed.

Four or five rebels tried to escape from the Alamo, hurtling over damaged walls. But they were seized by Mexican cavalrymen. All were quickly slain by Mexicans wielding knives or bayonets.

Some sources name Andrea Casteñon Ramirez Villanueva, known as Señora Candelaria, as yet another Alamo survivor. Señora Candelaria is said to have nursed Bowie in his final days. She was a *curandero,* a folk healer, using herbs, prayers, massage, and food, toys, and other gifts for the spirits, to perform cures.

Señora Candelaria claimed to have received from Sam Houston during the siege a letter that read, "Candelarita, go and take care of Bowie, my brother, in the Alamo." Señora Candelaria said she "took this as an order" and "obeyed immediately."

There are several versions of Bowie's last hours. The most popular declares that when Mexican soldiers burst into Bowie's sickroom they found the poor man sitting up in his bed, a pistol in each hand, and one of his famed knives in his lap. As the soldiers darted across the room to attack him, Bowie started firing, bringing down two of the soldiers with his pistol shots. Others plunged bayonets into him. But Bowie managed to knife a few of his attackers before he died. Legend has it that Mexican soldiers tossed Bowie's body into the air on the points of their bayonets.

Señora Candelaria offered a different version of Bowie's final moments. "I had hard work keeping Colonel Bowie in his bed," she said. "He got two pistols and began firing them off, shouting all the while to his men not to give up. He was raving. Finally, a bullet whizzed through the door, grazing my chin, and killed Bowie. I had the Colonel in my arms. I was giving him a drink."

According to Señora Candelaria, "Davy Crockett died fighting like a wild beast, within a few feet of me, and brave Colonel Travis within a few feet the other way. Poor Davy Crockett was killed near the entrance to the Church, his rifle in his hands. He was the last to die."

Señora Candelaria claimed to have been born in 1785. If that is true, she lived to a very old age, since she died in 1899. In the last decades of her life, she often entertained tourists with her colorful tales of the Alamo defenders.

CHAPTER 11

MASSACRE AT GOLIAD

Sam Houston, commander of the Texas army, was in Gonzales when he heard the shocking news that the Alamo had fallen. Travis had been shot to death. Bowie had been slain in bed. Crockett was one of a handful of rebels who had surrendered and been executed. The bodies of the Alamo defenders had been reduced to ashes on a massive pyre.

The waste of lives sickened Houston. He realized from the beginning that the efforts of the rebels to defend the Alamo were a sad misjudgment, the reason he had wanted the mission-fortress to be evacuated and destroyed.

Now Houston was concerned with Colonel Fannin at Mission La Bahía Fort Defiance at Goliad, where he commanded some 400 troops. Fort Defiance could be another Alamo, Houston believed, even though its hilltop location made it easier to defend. Houston wrote to Fannin, ordering him to blow up the fort and retreat to the town of Victoria on the Guadalupe River "as soon as practicable."

As commander of the rebel army, General Sam Houston proved to be a shrewd leader.

On March 13, Erastus "Deaf" Smith, on a scouting mission for Houston, found Susannah Dickinson and her daughter, Angelina, the Alamo survivors, on horseback on the road leading from San Antonio de Béxar and brought them back to Gonzales. Not only did Dickinson recount the horrifying details of the massacre at the Alamo, but she also brought the news that Santa Anna had unleashed his army to drive the rebels out of Texas. One unit of Mexican troops was already on the march from San Antonio de Béxar to Gonzales. They would arrive in a few days.

It didn't take long for Houston to react. He realized that the tiny army he commanded could not hope to successfully defend Gonzales, so that very night he ordered a retreat to the east, the beginning of an astonishing campaign that would eventually bring independence to Texas. Before leaving Gonzales, Houston ordered the town to be burned to the ground so that the Mexicans would find only ashes.

Cold rain fell steadily on Houston's army and the refugees from Gonzales as they marched east. Many of the men Houston commanded were property owners in Texas. When they heard the frightful news of the Alamo's fall and then learned that Santa Anna's army was on the march, more than a few of Houston's troops deserted, returning home to protect their families.

Houston's army reached the Colorado River, swollen as a result of the heavy rains, on March 17. Two days later, they pitched camp on the east bank. New

Though he had suffered a hearing loss, Erastus (Deaf) Smith was an outstanding scout and spy for the rebels.

groups of volunteers had joined the force. The Texan army now numbered more than 600 men.

On March 21, Houston received the news that the enemy force had arrived. Gen. Joaquín Ramírez y Sesma and his 700-man detachment were camped on the west bank of the Colorado River, only two miles north of Houston's encampment.

Houston decided that the time had come to make a stand and halt the Mexican advance. But then, on March 23, scouts arrived with crushing news concerning Fannin's army. Ordered by

Houston to evacuate the fortress in Goliad, Fannin had waited — and waited. When he finally decided to retreat, it was too late. Within a few miles of the fortress, his army had been overtaken and surrounded by a much larger Mexican force. Certain defeat loomed for Fannin and his men.

Houston now had to rethink his plans. With Fannin on the brink of surrender, Houston's army was the only one left to defend Texas. To attack Ramírez y Sesma's division on the other side of the Colorado made little sense now. Sesma had had time to build entrenchments. If he attacked and lost, the war itself would be lost. But even if he was successful in defeating Sesma's detachment, the victory might be costly and would mean little, for Houston would still have to contend with Santa Anna and the main body of the Mexican army.

Houston's decision was to keep retreating. He was prepared to march as

When Colonel Fannin and his troops left the safety of the Presidio La Bahía, what he called "Fort Defiance," they were quickly overtaken and captured by the Mexican army.

far east and north as necessary to find his best opportunity. As the troops set out, rain continued to pour down without letup. Houston's volunteers, tired of retreating, never stopped complaining. They grumbled wrongly that Houston was ready to retreat to Louisiana rather than defend Texas.

On the last day of March, Houston's army made camp on the west bank of Brazos River, where they were to rest and drill. While there, Houston learned what happened to poor Fannin. After surrendering to General José Francisco Urrea near Goliad, Fannin and his army of about 400 men were held captive for several days. On March 27, Mexican soldiers marched the prisoners out of Goliad, telling them that they were to be released. But Santa Anna had ordered their execution. The unarmed men were herded into long columns, made to kneel down, and then shot. Fannin himself was one of the victims. Twice as many rebels were massacred at Goliad as had died at the Alamo.

There were some survivors. The Mexicans spared about thirty individuals, the doctors, and some of the wounded. And another thirty or so men managed to escape by fleeing into the San Antonio River and nearby marshes under cover of the dense smoke from the rifles.

Texans were terrified by the news of the Mexican butchery at Goliad. Many settlers believed that Santa Anna's mission was to kill them all. In their panic, hundreds of settlers packed what belongings they could carry and left their homes to flee east toward the safety of American soil. Many of the refugees sickened and died in their flight. Later, Texans called this period of agony "the Runaway Scrape."

Meanwhile, Houston, with about 750 men now under his command, rested and drilled them. But Houston's troops didn't enjoy the game he was playing. Eager for combat, they were beginning to question their leader's courage. And David G. Burnet, the newly elected provisional president of Texas, was critical of him. "Sir," Burnet said in a letter to Houston, "The Enemy are laughing you to scorn. You must fight them. You must retreat no farther. The country expects you to fight."

On April 12, Houston learned that Santa Anna was passing through Fort Bend, heading farther east than Houston's encampment with a detachment of about 750 men, a force about equal to his own. Santa Anna had heard that Governor Burnet and other government officials had fled to Harrisburg, only thirty miles farther east beyond Fort Bend. Santa Anna hoped that by seizing the Texas leaders he could put a quick end to what remained of the rebellion.

Houston was happy to hear that Santa Anna was on the move toward Harrisburg. Here was an opportunity to meet the Mexican General on what seemed to be even terms. The next day, Houston moved his army across the Brazos to the east bank, then marched southeast, toward Harrisburg and Santa Anna.

But when Santa Anna reached

TEXAS!!

Emigrants who are desirious of assisting Texas at this important crisis of her affairs may have a free passage and equipments, by applying at the

NEW-YORK and PHILADELPHIA HOTEL,

On the Old Levee, near the Blue Stores.

Now is the time to ensure a fortune in Land: To all who remain in Texas during the War will be allowed 1280 Acres.

To all who remain Six Months, 640 Acres.

To all who remain Three Months, 320 Acres.

And as Colonists, 4600 Acres for a family and 1470 Acres for a Single Man.

New Orleans, April 23d, 1836.

"A fortune in land" was promised in exchange for service in Sam Houston's army.

Harrisburg, he found that Burnet and the other government officials had fled the day before aboard the steamer *Cayuga*. The vessel was headed down Buffalo Bayou to the San Jacinto River and from there to the town of New Washington and Galveston Bay. Santa Anna burned Harrisburg and quickly sent a band of cavalrymen to New Washington to seize the Texas leaders.

In New Washington, Santa Anna learned that Burnet and the Texas cabinet had escaped again. The Mexican leader was disappointed, but his chagrin faded as he completed his plans to double back and ambush Houston and his army, only ten miles away. Santa Anna was confident that when he sprung his trap he would end the revolution once and for all. So sure was the Mexican general of victory that he spent the next two days at rest.

Sam Houston was not resting. He marched his army sixty miles in two and a half days, arriving at Buffalo Bayou, just across from Harrisburg, at midday on April 18. The next day, Houston addressed his men. He told them that the Mexican army was a short distance away and they were soon to fight. "Victory is certain!" he cried. "Trust in God and fear not. The victims of the Alamo and the names of those murdered at Goliad cry out for vengeance. Remember the Alamo! Remember Goliad!"

After crossing Buffalo Bayou by means of Vince's Bridge and marching another eight miles, Houston's army reached an open plain known as San Jacinto, which was surrounded on three sides by swampland. It was here that Santa Anna planned to trap Houston. But it was Santa Anna who would be trapped.

For weeks, Houston's troops had been thirsting for combat. They now knew they did not have long to wait. Morale soared.

CHAPTER 12

VICTORY AND VENGEANCE

Houston ordered his men to camp along Buffalo Bayou near the point where it joined the San Jacinto River at Lynch's Ferry. Groves of live oak draped with gray Spanish moss skirted the bayou. Houston's men concealed themselves in the thick growth.

Santa Anna was on the way. After burning New Washington, the Mexican general had set out for Lynch's Ferry, where he planned to lie in wait for Houston's army. He was surprised to find that Houston was already there. He ordered his artillerymen to bring up a six-pound cannon and begin firing. Houston's men answered back with fire from two six-pounders, which they had nicknamed the Twin Sisters. The two sides also exchanged some rifle fire.

Santa Anna hoped he could lure the Texans out into the open, but they would not budge, remaining hidden, and firing from the trees. Santa Anna then withdrew his troops and made camp for the night in a wooded area on the banks of the San Jacinto. Less than a half a mile separated the two armies across an open plain carpeted in prairie grass.

Thursday, April 21, 1836, was a bright, sunshine-filled day. Around nine o'clock in the morning loud cheers came from the Mexican camp. General Cós had arrived with several hundred reinforcements. The arrivals boosted Santa Anna's army to something more than 1,200 men.

Since there was no sign of activity in Houston's camp, Santa Anna had his men stack their arms. Then he ordered them to build a barricade out of sacks of supplies and pack saddles as a defense against a surprise attack. Afternoon passed with no attack; the Mexicans rested. The cavalrymen unsaddled and watered their horses. Santa Anna napped.

In the rebels' camp, the soldiers fretted. They had risen early, expecting to be ordered into action at dawn, but no order had come. Houston had slept, not rising until eight o'clock. He shrugged when told that General Cós had arrived

Titled "Massacre at Peggy's Lake," this historic painting by Charles Shaw shows the fury of the Texans' attack.

with reinforcements for Santa Anna. Better they arrive now, he said, than during the battle.

One of Houston's first moves that morning was to send "Deaf" Smith and a handful of riders on a mission to destroy Vince's Bridge, to chop it down or burn it. The rebels had used it earlier to gain access to what was to be the battlefield, as had General Cós's men. "It cut off all means of escape for either army," Houston was to note later. "There was no alternative but victory or death."

Around two o'clock in the afternoon, Houston sent Col. Joseph Bennett through the ranks to assess the mood of the men. He found the rebels ready — fed, rested, their weapons loaded, eager for battle. It would be hard to hold them back any longer.

At 3:30, while Santa Anna still slept, Houston ordered his army to assemble.

They formed an attacking line, two men deep, several hundred yards long, in front of the wooded area where they had camped.

At Houston's order, the long line surged forward. Houston rode up and down the length of the line on a white stallion. Many of the Mexicans were resting, unaware the attack had begun. No sentinels alerted them. "Hold your fire, men!" Houston called out, "Hold your fire!" The men began moving on the run.

When the rebel line got to within 200 yards of the Mexican camp, Houston signaled for the cannons to be fired. As his troops rushed toward the Mexican camp, cries of "Remember the Alamo!" and "Remember Goliad!" echoed up and down the line.

Once the rebels started to shoot, they did not stop. "All discipline was at an

This towering monument now marks site of battle of San Jacinto.

killed every one they caught. Many of them were unarmed; some of them were already wounded. By Houston's own estimate, the battle lasted eighteen minutes. But the slaughter went on for hours. Some 650 Mexicans were killed. Nine of Houston's men lost their lives.

Santa Anna escaped on horseback. The next morning a search party found the Mexican general, but they were unaware who he was. When he was brought back to camp, Mexican prisoners, 300 of whom had been rounded up after the killing stopped, called out, "El Presidente! El Presidente!" The rebel Texans knew at once the identity of their captive.

Santa Anna asked to meet the leader of the rebel army. When the Mexican leader was brought to him, Sam Houston was lying beneath an oak tree, in great pain. A rifle bullet had shattered his right ankle in the early stages of the battle.

Under the oak, the two men struck a bargain. Houston feared the thousands of Mexican troops still in Texas. A force of 2,500, under the command of Gen. Vicente Filisola, was only two or three days away. Houston realized that his men, fatigued from long marches and battle, would be no match for the

end," Priv. Alphonso Steele wrote. "We fired as rapidly as we could. As soon as we had fired, each man reloaded and he who got his gun ready first moved out without waiting for orders."

Yelling, with rifles and long knives in their hands, the rebels swarmed over the flimsy barricade the Mexicans had built and into their camp, where all was confusion. Many Mexican troops fled in uncontrolled panic. Those who remained were shot or knifed to death.

Houston and his officers were unable to control their crazed troops. The rebels chased down the fleeing Mexicans and

Mexican force of that size.

Santa Anna was fearful, too. Reminded by Houston of how the Mexicans had massacred rebel prisoners at Goliad, Santa Anna was afraid he might be executed.

So it was the two men came to a simple arrangement. Houston promised to spare Santa Anna's life if the Mexican leader would order all of his remaining forces out of Texas. Santa Anna wasted no time in ordering Filisola to pull the Mexican army back into Mexico.

Within a month, the negotiations between Houston and Santa Anna that had been conducted under the oak tree were set down in two treaties, one secret, one public — the Treaties of Velasco, as they are called. According to their terms, Santa Anna recognized Texas to be an independent state and promised never to take up arms again against Texas.

The revolution was over. Texas was free of Mexico — or at least Texans thought they were.

Sam Houston (at base of tree) discusses surrender terms with Santa Anna. Deaf Smith, one hand cupped to his ear, is at Houston's left.

CHAPTER 13

STATEHOOD FOR TEXAS

The years following Houston's victory at San Jacinto were troublesome ones for Texas, partly because Mexico did not recognize Texas as an independent nation. Nevertheless, a permanent government with Houston as president came into power in October 1836.

Houston faced a wide range of challenges, including internal rivalries and an empty treasury. Many people saw a union with the United States as a solution to the problems.

Texas joined the United States in 1845. Mexico, still claiming Texas, ended diplomatic relations with the United States. After a border skir-

In September 1836, less than six months after the battle of San Jacinto, Sam Houston, winning some 80 percent of the vote, was elected Texas's first president. In later years, he served as a U.S. senator from Texas and governor of the state.

mish, President James K. Polk claimed Mexico had invaded American territory. In May 1846, the United States declared war on Mexico.

Mexicans were shocked. They called the Mexican War "the United States invasion of Mexico."

U.S. forces occupied Mexican territory in what is now Arizona, California, and New Mexico. Other American troops captured Mexico City. Not long after, Mexico surrendered.

The conflict ended with the Treaty of Guadalupe Hidalgo, signed on February 2, 1848. Under the terms of the treaty, Mexico gave up nearly half of its territory — the land that is

A demonstration in Jersey City, New Jersey, in 1845, in support of the Mexican War. "Texas Shall Be Ours," a banner declares.

now California, Nevada, and Utah, most of Arizona, and parts of Colorado, New Mexico, and Wyoming. Mexico also gave up all claims to Texas north of the Rio Grande. In return, the United States paid Mexico $15 million.

Five years later, in what is called the Gadsden Purchase, the United States gave Mexico $10 million for what is now southern New Mexico and Arizona.

The Treaty of Guadalupe Hidalgo settled matters between the United States and Mexico, but Texas's boundaries were still in question. Texas claimed much of the land in the southwestern United States that had been acquired from Mexico. In 1850 the federal government agreed to pay Texas $10 million to give up its claims. The boundaries of Texas were then permanently fixed and its U.S. statehood as we know it began.

VOLUNTEERS !

During the Mexican War, a $30 bonus and 160 acres of Texas land were promised to volunteers from the state of New Hampshire.

CHAPTER 14

THE ALAMO TODAY

There's not much left of the original Alamo. The three-acre walled-in complex of 1836, with its several buildings for housing soldiers, its chapel, and other structures arranged around an open plaza, no longer exists. A Wendy's fast-food restaurant, a visitor information center, and Uncle Hoppy's "Bar-B-Cue" now stand on the western fringe of what was once the Alamo compound. Santa Anna's attack on the Alamo in 1836 started from what is now the swimming pool of the Crockett Hotel.

What has survived are two structures — the chapel and the Long Barracks. The chapel and the artifacts displayed there now serve as a memorial to the Alamo's rebel defenders. It is known as "The Shrine of Texas Liberty." The Long Barracks, restored in 1968, is now a museum. The Alamo compound today also includes a large building that serves as a museum and souvenir shop. There's a library for historical research in the southwest corner of the complex.

The chapel and Long Barracks are fortunate to have escaped destruction. After the battle of the Alamo, when Santa Anna began mapping plans to subdue what remained of the rebel army, he placed Gen. Juan José Andrade in charge of San Antonio de Béxar. General Andrade's assignment was to keep open Santa Anna's lines of supply and care for wounded Mexican soldiers.

General Andrade was still in command at San Antonio at the time of Santa Anna's defeat at San Jacinto. Like Filisola and the other Mexican generals, Andrade was told to pull back his army into Mexico. Before departing, Andrade ordered his men to destroy the Alamo. They ransacked the buildings, tore down walls, and set fire to the chapel, a blaze that left only the thick masonry walls standing. In the years that followed, the abandoned structures baked in the hot Texas sun and were ravaged by the wind and rain. To San Antonio children, the ruins became a playground.

The Alamo in 1846, from a drawing that appeared in Gleason's Pictorial.

In 1847 the U.S. Army took over the Alamo. During the Mexican War (1846–1848), the army reclaimed the chapel, cleared out the debris, and began to use it as a warehouse. It was during this period that the army added the distinctive hump atop the Alamo's west facade. The U.S. Army used the Long Barracks for storage, too. The structure also served as a shelter for horses.

During the Civil War (1861–1865), when San Antonio was in the hands of Confederate forces, the Alamo was the headquarters and drill center for a company of local militia. The U.S. Army took over the building again when the Civil War ended.

In 1883 the state of Texas purchased

Clara Driscoll, a descendant of a veteran of the Battle of San Jacinto, contributed funds to help preserve the Alamo. She later served two terms as state president of The Daughters of the Republic of Texas.

The Long Barracks, the oldest of the Alamo's buildings, once contained living quarters for priests, a kitchen, and a dining room. Today, it's a museum.

the Alamo chapel and turned it over to the city of San Antonio. The Long Barracks, which had become a commercial building, was purchased by the Daughters of the Republic of Texas through the efforts of its president Adina de Zavala and Clara Driscoll, a descendant of a veteran of the Battle of San Jacinto. Since 1905, the buildings have been administered and cared for by the Daughters of the Republic of Texas.

The Daughters of the Republic of Texas have also sought to control the story of the Alamo and what took place there. In this regard they've been criticized. It's been said that they have done little to set forth the mission's history before 1836 and that they have ignored or downplayed the role of Tejanos as defenders of the Alamo. Native Americans say that the Alamo contains important history that has been overlooked.

The Alamo attracts some 13,000 visitors a day, many of them in school groups.

In recent years, however, closer ties between the United States and Mexico and the increasing influence of Texas's millions of Hispanics are helping to bring about change. Historians no longer describe the Texas Revolution as a cultural conflict between oppressive Mexicans and freedom-loving Americans.

"The doors have been opened," says William Thornton, who became mayor of San Antonio in 1995. "Places have been made at the table for people whose voices have not been heard before."

Important Dates in Alamo History and Texas's Struggle for Independence

1519
Alonso Álvarez de Piñeda maps the Gulf Coast from Florida to Mexico, claiming the land for Spain.

1528
Spain's Álvar Núñez Cabeza de Vaca, is shipwrecked on the Gulf Coast and later explores Texas to western Mexico.

1541
Francisco Vásquez de Coronado of Spain explores part of west Texas from New Mexico.

1542
Hernando de Soto's Spanish expedition, now led by Luís Moscoso de Alvarado, explores part of northeast Texas.

1682
Spanish friars establish first two missions in Texas near what is now the city of El Paso.

1685
France's René-Robert Cavelier, Sieur de La Salle, establishes Fort St. Louis on Matagorda Bay.

1690
Spanish establish two missions, later abandoned, in east Texas.

1718
Franciscan friars establish Mission San Antonio de Valero (later known as the Alamo) on west bank of San Antonio River.

1756
Construction starts on what is to become the present Alamo chapel.

1801
The Second Flying Company of San Carlos del Álamo de Parras occupies Mission Valero, leading to the naming of the site as "the Alamo."

1821

Mexico gains its independence from Spain. Texas becomes a part of the new empire of Mexico.

1824

Mexico becomes a republic. The Mexican state of Texas is combined with the state of Coahuila and the state capital is moved from San Antonio de Béxar to Saltillo.

1830

Mexico prohibits further colonization in Texas as well as the importation of slaves. Taxes are assessed for the first time and their collection is enforced by army garrisons.

1833

Gen. Antonio López de Santa Anna becomes Mexico's president on April 1. Also on April 1, in a convention of Texans at San Felipe de Austin, delegates petition Mexico City to reopen the borders and for statehood. A draft constitution for the new state is written. Stephen F. Austin goes to Mexico City with the resolutions.

1835

Santa Anna establishes himself as Mexico's dictator and abolishes the Constitution of 1824.

June 29: Armed Texans under William Barret Travis expel troops from a Mexican garrison at Anahuac.

October 2: The Texas Revolution begins near the town of Gonzales when a rebel force of 150 volunteers opens fire on a Mexican cavalry unit, forcing the Mexicans to retreat.

October 9: A band of rebels forces the surrender of a Mexican military garrison at the old Mission La Bahía in Goliad.

October 13: Texan rebels begin march to San Antonio de Béxar. Under the command of Stephen Austin the rebels sit at siege for weeks.

November 3: Delegates to the Consultation, the second convention at San Felipe de Austin, vote to remain a part of Mexico and fight for the reestablishment of the Constitution of 1824.

December 5–9: A rebel force attacks and captures the Mexican strongholds of San Antonio de Béxar and the Alamo, forcing the surrender of Gen. Martín Perfecto de Cós.

1836

January 26: General Santa Anna, commanding an army of more than 4,000 troops, begins the march north into Texas from Coahuila to subdue Texas's rebels.

February 23–March 6: Santa Anna's army lays siege to the Alamo, overpowering the rebel defenders.

March 2: Texans, meeting at Washington-on-the-Brazos, approve a declaration of independence and frame a constitution.

March 18–27: A rebel force of about 400 men under Col. James Walker Fannin surrenders to Mexican troops at Goliad. The rebels are then assassinated by order of Santa Anna.

April 21: Sam Houston's troops defeat Santa Anna's army in the Battle of San Jacinto. Texas declares its independence from Mexico.

1845
December 29: Texas becomes the twenty-eighth state of the United States.

1846–1848
The United States defeats Mexico in the Mexican War.

1850
In the compromise of 1850, Texas's dispute with the federal government over the New Mexico Territory is resolved and the state's western border is established.

1861
Civil War erupts in April. Alamo is occupied by Confederate Army.

1883
Alamo chapel sold by Catholic Church to the state of Texas.

1905
State of Texas assigns Daughters of the Republic of Texas to operate and maintain the Alamo.

FOR FURTHER READING

Young Readers

Barr, Alwyn. *Texans in Revolt: The Battle for San Antonio, 1835*. Austin: University of Texas Press, 1990.

Evans, Barbara Stanush. *Texans: A Story of Texan Cultures for Young People*. San Antonio: University of Texas Institute of Texan Cultures, 1988.

Fisher, Leonard Everett. *The Alamo*. New York: Holiday House, 1987.

Fritz, Jean. *Make Way for Sam Houston*. New York: G. P. Putnam's, 1986.

Hauch, Richard Boyd. *Davy Crockett: A Handbook*. Lincoln, Neb.: University of Nebraska Press, 1986.

Kerr, Rita. *Juan Seguín: A Hero for Texas*. Austin: Eakin Press, 1985.

Matthews, Cahndice E. *Gregorio Esparza, Alamo Hero*. Austin: Eakin Press, 1995.

Ragsdale, Crystal Sasse. *The Women and Children of the Alamo*. Austin: State House Press, 1992.

Stein, R. Conrad. *The Story of the Lone Star Republic*. Chicago: Children's Press, 1989.

Warren, Betsy. *Indians Who Lived in Texas*. Dallas: Hendrik-Long, 1981.

Young-Adult Readers

Binkley, William C. *The Texas Revolution*. Baton Rouge: Louisiana State University Press, 1952.

Castañeda, Carlos. *The Mexican Side of the Texas Revolution*. Dallas: P. L. Turner Co., 1928.

Chariton, Wallace O. *Exploring the Alamo Legends*. Plano, Tex.: Worldwide Publishing, 1992.

Crawford, Ann Fears, editor. *The Autobiography of Santa Anna*. Austin: State House Press, 1988.

Fehrenbach, T. R. *Lone Star: A History of Texas and the Texans*. New York: Macmillan, 1968.

Frantz, Joe B. *Texas: A Bicentennial History*. New York: W. W. Norton, 1976.

Long, Jeff. *Duel of Eagles*. New York: Morrow, 1990.

Lord, Walter. *A Time to Stand*. New York: Harper & Brothers, 1961.

Nevin, David. *The Texans*. New York: Time-Life Books, 1975.

Newcomb, W. W., Jr. *The Indians of Texas*. Austin: University of Texas Press, 1961.

Santos, Richard G. *Santa Anna's Campaign Against Texas: 1835–1836*. Waco, Tex.: Texian Press, 1967.

Tinkle, Lon. *Thirteen Days to Glory*. New York: McGraw-Hill, 1958.

INDEX

INTERIOR PHOTO CREDITS